THIS BOOK BELONGS TO

_ _ _ _ _ _ _ _ _ _ _ _ _ _

First published in the UK in 2021 and in the US in 2022
by Tiny Owl Publishing, London

For teacher resources and more information, visit
www.tinyowl.co.uk
#TinyOwlCelebrate

A catalogue record for this book is available from the British Library.
A CIP record for this book is available from the Library of Congress.

UK ISBN 9781910328675
US ISBN 9781910328897

Printed in China

We all Celebrate!

Chitra Soundar

Jenny Bloomfield

TINY OWL

We all celebrate!

We celebrate to mark birthdays and weddings, the onset of seasons, and to thank nature for a bountiful harvest. We celebrate religious festivals, national holidays, and to seek blessings from our ancestors.

Many celebratory traditions and rituals have evolved over centuries, and they are often full of colour, special foods, and plenty of laughter and joy.

Celebrations and Calendars

Celebrations take place throughout the year. This is the modern-day Gregorian calendar. It has 365 days, starting on January 1st and finishing on December 31st. Every four years, an extra day is added to February to make it a leap year. This keeps the calendar in alignment with the revolutions of the Sun.

A lunar calendar is based on the monthly cycles of the moon. A lunar month could be 29 or 30 days. This means there are only 354 or 355 days in a lunar year. The lunar calendar shapes the lives and celebrations of many communities around the world.

JANUARY
M T W T F S S
          1 2
3 4 5 6 7 8 9
10 11 12 13 14 15 16
17 18 19 20 21 22 23
24 25 26 27 28 29 30
31

FEBRUARY
M T W T F S S
      1 2 3 4 5 6
7 8 9 10 11 12 13
14 15 16 17 18 19 20
21 22 23 24 25 26 27
28

MARCH
M T W T F S S
      1 2 3 4 5 6
7 8 9 10 11 12 13
14 15 16 17 18 19 20
21 22 23 24 25 26 27
28 29 30 31

APRIL
M T W T F S S
          1 2 3
4 5 6 7 8 9 10
11 12 13 14 15 16 17
18 19 20 21 22 23 24
25 26 27 28 29 30

MAY
M T W T F S S
            1
2 3 4 5 6 7 8
9 10 11 12 13 14 15
16 17 18 19 20 21 22
23 24 25 26 27 28 29
30 31

JUNE
M T W T F S S
      1 2 3 4 5
6 7 8 9 10 11 12
13 14 15 16 17 18 19
20 21 22 23 24 25 26
27 28 29 30

JULY
M T W T F S S
          1 2 3
4 5 6 7 8 9 10
11 12 13 14 15 16 17
18 19 20 21 22 23 24
25 26 27 28 29 30 31

AUGUST
M T W T F S S
1 2 3 4 5 6 7
8 9 10 11 12 13 14
15 16 17 18 19 20 21
22 23 24 25 26 27 28
29 30 31

SEPTEMBER
M T W T F S S
      1 2 3 4
5 6 7 8 9 10 11
12 13 14 15 16 17 18
19 20 21 22 23 24 25
26 27 28 29 30

OCTOBER
M T W T F S S
          1 2
3 4 5 6 7 8 9
10 11 12 13 14 15 16
17 18 19 20 21 22 23
24 25 26 27 28 29 30
31

NOVEMBER
M T W T F S S
1 2 3 4 5 6
7 8 9 10 11 12 13
14 15 16 17 18 19 20
21 22 23 24 25 26 27
28 29 30

DECEMBER
M T W T F S S
      1 2 3 4
5 6 7 8 9 10 11
12 13 14 15 16 17 18
19 20 21 22 23 24 25
26 27 28 29 30 31

Sun

As the Earth rotates around the sun, when the northern hemisphere tilts closer to the sun, the southern hemisphere is away from it.
So when the northern hemisphere gets summer, the southern hemisphere gets winter.
People therefore celebrate during different times.
Still, we all celebrate!

Northern Hemisphere

Moon

Equator

Southern Hemisphere

The start of a Year

Happy cheers of "Happy new year!" signal the start of another year as people wish one another good fortune for the year ahead with large parties and huge fireworks lighting up the skies.

In **Canada,** people jump into the cold sea to mark the new year by doing the *Polar Bear Plunge.* It's catching on in other countries, too.

BRRRrrrr

In **Greece,** a coin is hidden inside a special cake called *vasilopita,* to bring good luck to one lucky finder.

In **Scotland,** *Hogmanay* is celebrated the day before New Year when families clean their houses from top to bottom. Then, before midnight everyone stands outside their house. When the bells ring in the new year, family and friends sing *Auld Lang Syne* while a tall, dark, and handsome guest is invited to enter the home first. This is called the first-footing, and this friend usually carries in coal for the fire to bring luck for the coming year.

Nowruz Pirooz!

Not all calendars start on January 1st. Nowruz, the Persian New Year, is celebrated in March when day and night are of equal lengths.

Nowruz is celebrated across many countries including **Iran, Uzbekistan, Tajikistan, Afghanistan, Azerbaijan, Kazakhstan, Kyrgyzstan,** and **Turkmenistan.**

On the eve of the last Wednesday before Nowruz, Persians celebrate Chaharshanbe Suri – the festival of fire – by building a fire and jumping over it.

A day before the festival, everyone gets together to paint eggs in vibrant colours to place them on *haft-seen*, the ceremonial table.

sumac (crushed spice of berries, for sunrise and the spice of life)

senjed (sweet dry lotus berries, for love and affection)

seeb (apples, for health and beauty)

sir (garlic, for good health)

serkeh (vinegar, for patience and age)

sabzeh (sprouted wheat grass, for rebirth and renewal of nature)

samanu (wheat pudding, for fertility and sweetness of life)

In India, the traditional new year celebration is also marked during the spring season. The celebrations are known by a different name in different parts of the country – *Ugadhi, Baisakhi, Puthandu, and Vishu.*

The Queen of Sheba

Far away in **Ethiopia**, New Year, called *Enkutatash* (the gift of jewels), is celebrated on September 12th. It marks the end of the rainy season, when the countryside is covered with yellow daisies. On this day, people also remember the jewels that were presented to the Queen of Sheba when she returned from her trip to Jerusalem 3,000 years ago.

Xin Nián Kuài Lè!

In **China** and other parts of South East Asia, the Lunar New Year is celebrated over two weeks, and it usually takes place in January or February. During this fortnight, families get together to thank their gods and ancestors. Neighbourhoods and houses are decorated often with red decorations as a symbol of luck.

Every Lunar year has a zodiac animal of its own. There are 12 zodiac animals–Rat, Ox, Tiger, Rabbit, Dragon, Snake, Horse, Goat, Monkey, Rooster, Dog, and Pig. Can you find out your Lunar zodiac from the year you were born?

In Chinese families, elders bless their children by giving them money in red packeats called *hóngbāo*.

Lunar New Year celebrations usually end with the Lantern festival. Everyone gathers to watch lion and dragon dances on the streets. At night, families meet to light paper lanterns and send them high into the sky.

Spring

All over the world, countries hold celebrations to welcome the season of spring. It's the time of year when thick sweaters and coats can be put away, and flowers begin to bloom, bursting with colour.

In **Japan**, people gather for Hanami—to look at and appreciate the beauty of the sakura, or cherry blossoms. They welcome spring by meeting friends under the trees bursting with the delicate pink sakura.

In **Bulgaria**, Granny March or Baba Marta arrives on March 1st, bringing to an end the cold winter and marking the start of spring. On this day, Bulgarians wear martenitsi bracelets made of white and red yarn that are worn until a sign of spring—a stork or swallow—is spotted. Then they are placed on a tree or under a rock as a symbol of hope for the year ahead.

BANG!

BANG!

In some parts of **India**, spring is welcomed with Holi, the festival of colors, where colored powder and water is thrown, and people dance to music.

Venture into Valencia in **Spain**, by the Mediterranean coast in March, and people are putting up giant ninots, or papier-mache figures, during the Las Fallas festival.

People compete to put up giant wooden figures called ninots. This comes from a carpenter's tradition of burning wood when winter leaves and spring arrives. Judges come around to view all the ninots and the best one, *ninot induldat*, is chosen. Only the ninot induldat is saved and the rest are thrown into the bonfire.

When the parade ends, firecrackers are lit one after the other, leading to a BIG BANG! A mighty explosion rocks the center of the city when all the firecrackers go off at the same time to celebrate the start of spring and commemorate San Jose, the patron saint of carpentry.

Summer

When the Earth tilts toward the Sun, the hemisphere facing it gets the longest day of the year, celebrated as the Summer Solstice.

In **Sweden,** families gather in open countryside and parks to celebrate this day as the Midsummer Festival. It's a day to make flower garlands, decorate the maypole, and bask in the sunshine.

In the **United Kingdom,** people gather at Stonehenge in England and at the Ring of Brodgar on the Orkney Islands to welcome in the warm summer months. At Stonehenge, when the sun rises behind the Heel stone and its first rays stream into the center of the famous stone monument, the gathered crowd cheers.

Children and grown-ups compete in egg and spoon races, dance around the maypole to the *Små grodorna* song, also called the Little Frogs song, and challenge each other in a tug of war.

Pickled herring, boiled potatoes, and a big helping of fresh strawberries with cream makes for a great midsummer feast.

Fasting

Across the world, many religions teach fasting as a time of reflection and prayer.

Healthy adult **Muslims** worldwide observe a month-long fast during Ramadan, the ninth lunar month of the Islamic calendar. Each fasting day begins before sunrise with the pre-dawn meal of suhur. It is an important meal that will help in staying hydrated and give lots of energy throughout the day of fasting. During the fast, no drinking or eating is allowed. The fast is broken with a meal called the iftar at sunset.

The first day of the next month is known as Eid al-Fitr—the festival of breaking the fast. Muslims celebrate by cleaning and decorating their homes, buying new clothes, and enjoying a feast together. Elders give money as gifts to children in their family to mark the occasion.

Hindus and Buddhist traditions include fasting on special days of prayer or giving up eating meat on certain days, too.

Jewish families also fast and pray during Yom Kippur, which is the holiest day of the year in the Jewish calendar.

Many Christians fast during Lent, which lasts for 40 days. While some give up meat, eggs, or alcohol, others fast on special days of prayer like Ash Wednesday or Good Friday.

Carnivals

Carnivals are huge celebrations that take place in many different countries around the world each year.

In the past, Catholic Christians celebrated the upcoming religious fast during Lent with a carnival of music, parades, and feasts.

As Catholic European countries colonized and enslaved other parts of the world, they brought the carnival celebrations to people in South America and the Caribbean.

The enslaved people were forbidden to celebrate their own traditions and customs, but many found ways to merge their celebrations with the carnival to keep their culture alive.

After World War II, over half a million people from Trinidad and Tobago, Jamaica, Barbados, Guyana, and other Caribbean countries came to work in the United Kingdom. But, in the 1940s, British people weren't very accepting of immigrants.

In **West London** in 1959, Claudia Jones, an immigrant from Trinidad & Tobago, brought the Afro-Caribbean community together in an indoor carnival in St. Pancras Town Hall. It was televised and people across Britain watched the music and dancing of the people from Trinidad & Tobago and other Afro-Caribbean nations.

In South America, the carnival at Rio de Janeiro in **Brazil** is held before Lent and is one of the biggest carnivals in the world. Tourists come to experience this spectacular event, complete with samba dancers competing in the Sambodromo and crowded street parties.

Claudia Jones' indoor carnival grew to become the Notting Hill Carnival, one of the biggest in the world. Today, it is Europe's largest street festival, celebrated across a weekend in the summer month of August.

The highlight of the outdoor celebrations is the steelpan drums played by different bands set up along the street.

JERK CHICKEN

Did you know steelpan drums were originally fashioned out of old oil drums by musicians from Trinidad & Tobago?

Island Festivals

The Pacific Ocean has many small islands, separated by vast expanses of sea. Distanced from one another and set apart from the rest of the world, these islands and their festivals are truly unique.

In Samoa, spring is the time to celebrate the Teuila Festival. Named after their national flower red ginger, pronounced te-oo-wee-lah, this festival honors the ancient traditions of the Samoan tribes.

During the week-long celebrations, people watch the fire-knife dance called the Siva afi. This dance demonstrates the ancient warfare methods of the tribes. Don't get too close!

Music and dance troops participate in competitions, and artisans show off their traditional arts and crafts.

Indonesia is a country of many islands and ancient tribes in the Pacific Ocean. On the Indonesian island of Lombok, the Sasak people celebrate the festival of Bau Nyale in February or March to remember Princess Mandalika who jumped into the sea to save them.

Long ago, Princess Mandalika was known for her beauty. Princes from all over the islands battled with each other to marry her. This made the princess very unhappy. She fell into the open sea and was transformed into an abundance of sea worms. People of Lombok believe that Princess Mandalika lives forever in the form of the sea worm, known locally as nyale, and she returns to the island every year to bless them.

To this day, the people of Lombok catch and eat the nyale, to bring them good fortune.

Food Festivals

Many festivals and celebrations involve food being served and eaten in a special way but some festivals use it in a very different way!

In late August 1945, a parade was taking place in the town of Bunol in **Spain**, with people dressed as giants with big heads. A group of young people caused someone's giant head to fall off and a fight broke out. One young man threw a tomato at his friends.

Next year, the parade was forgotten but the tomato fight was not and La Tomatina was born.

Some years later, when the police tried to stop the now annual tomato fight, the young men re-enacted a "funeral parade" by carrying a coffin containing a giant tomato.

Not to be beaten, the **Australians** celebrate with melons. Every two years, at the Chinchilla Melon Festival, melons are weighed, eaten, smashed, thrown, and celebrated for a whole week.

The people in Bessières in **France** don't throw fruit at each other. Instead, they break over 15,000 eggs to make a giant omelette. It's called ... you guessed it, The Giant Omelette Festival.

SQUASH -SPLAT !

Soon, all of Spain and the rest of the world found out about this fun food festival. Every year, during the summer, people gather to throw tomatoes at each other to celebrate this messy and juicy festival.

Celebrating in the South

To mark the start of the new year, the Maori people of **New Zealand** celebrate Nga mata o te ariki o Tawhirimatea, which means "the eye of the god of Tawhirimatea" and is shortened to Matariki. It is a time of growth and change. Matariki is the name for a cluster of stars that rise in mid-winter (June/July) and signals the start of a new year.

The Maori people take time to thank the harvest that has gone the year before, and people celebrate with family and friends, share food, sing songs, dance the haka (an ancient Maori war dance), and offer the harvest to the god of food, Rongo.

In the last two decades, this festival has grown to be celebrated across New Zealand as Aotearoa Pacific New Year, creating new traditions with fireworks, tree planting, and family feasts.

The multi-ethnic community in the western Cape region of **South Africa** has customs and traditions which reflect the multiple cultures of their ancestors, and their celebrations tell a story.

Before slavery was abolished in 1834, slaves were given just one holiday a year—January 2nd. On this day, they celebrated a carnival called Kaapse Klopse or Tweede Nuwe jaar, by wearing bright colors and playing music. Their music was a melting pot of their diverse cultures—from the local Bantu people to those who had been brought from South Asia and South East Asia.

After slavery was abolished, people in Cape Town continued to celebrate this holiday to keep the spirit of freedom alive. Troops, including children, perform music, dances and other variety shows in this minstrel carnival.

Lwiindi Gonde is a thanksgiving ceremony celebrated every year by the Tonga people in **Zambia** to give thanks to the first harvest and to their first chief fondly called Mukukulukulu who they believe is the bringer of rains. It takes place in the Gonde, in Chief Monze's palace, during the first weekend of July.

Autumn

When the summer sun begins to fade, people turn their attention to the warm colors of autumn and herald in a new season with elaborate celebrations and festivities.

Hindus around the world mark the festival of Deepavali over five days, by lighting lamps and celebrating the eternal victory of good over evil. This festival is always celebrated as the waning moon disappears and the new moon rises in the middle of the lunar month of Karthika. Each of the five days are dedicated to different celebrations.

Although customs and traditions vary across communities, most Hindus will wear new clothes, decorate their homes with lights, exchange gifts, and share candy with neighbours and friends. While those from the north of India will light lamps on the new moon's night, people in the south start celebrations before the sun rises at dawn.

During the five day festival, fireworks are lit. Families get together for feasts and send greeting cards to near and dear ones.

In September during the Hungry Ghosts festival, it's believed that the gates of the afterlife are thrown open and the spirits of the dead can roam the Earth. Buddhists and Taoists in South East Asia honor their dead relatives and ancestors. The main ceremony takes place at dusk when ancestral possessions are placed on the table, a feast is eaten, and sometimes a place is left empty at the table for a lost ancestor.

In Mexico, people remember their ancestors in November during Día de los Muertos. Over two days of celebrations, families pay respects to the dead and believe their ancestors will return to Earth. The festival is an explosion of colour. Revellers put on distinctive make-up and costumes, hold parades, dance, and make offerings to lost relatives.

Winter

In **Peru**, people celebrate the winter solstice in the middle of June, in a celebration called Inti Raymi, by offering prayers to the sun god Inti and Mother Earth, Pachamama.

The traditional celebrations last nine days and include colourful costumes and share traditional foods and playing music.

Chanukah, the festival of the Miracle of Oil is celebrated by Jewish people across the world in early winter to remember the time when the lamp in the Temple in Jerusalem burned for eight days even though it had just enough oil to last a day.

Over eight days and nights, a menorah is lighted with the first candle called the shamash. Then each night, one more candle is lit using the shamash until all the candles are burning brightly. Some families exchange presents, while others gift their children with Chanukah gelt or money during this festival.

Traditional fried food, cooked in oil, such as Sufganiyot (doughnuts) or latkes (potato pancakes) are enjoyed during this festival, too.

Christmas

Christmas is a time of joy and celebration for many people from different cultures around the world. Each has its own traditions and festivities.

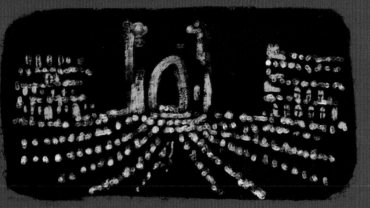

Colombia begins Christmas with The Day of the Little Candles on December 8th. People place lit candles and paper lanterns outside their homes and balconies.

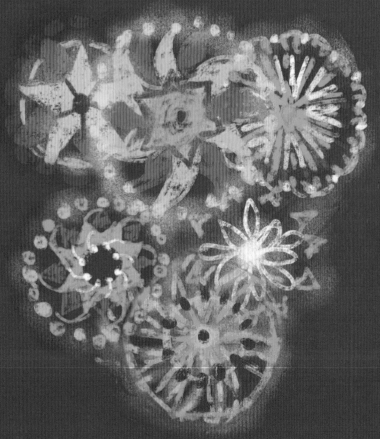

In many western countries, families hang wreaths on their doors, bring Christmas trees into their homes, and decorate the trees with lights, tinsel, and ornaments.

In San Fernando in the Philippines, The Giant Lantern Festival is celebrated around the time of Christmas. Teams compete to create huge lantern displays called parols that signify hope and commemorate the star of Bethlehem.

While many celebrate Christmas on December 25th to mark the birth of Jesus Christ, others celebrate the same occasion on January 5th or 6th.

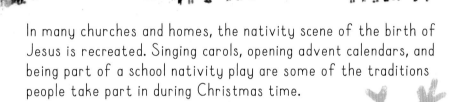

In many churches and homes, the nativity scene of the birth of Jesus is recreated. Singing carols, opening advent calendars, and being part of a school nativity play are some of the traditions people take part in during Christmas time.

Across the world,
on Christmas Eve, children leave treats like pies or cookies, and a drink for Santa Claus and carrots for his reindeer.

For some, Christmas Day starts with the opening of presents. Others attend a mass at church. Families usually gather for a special Christmas meal to celebrate.

Celebrations bring us together
with music, dance, and feasts.
Our celebrations are not
only steeped in customs and
traditions, they also change
and evolve as we do.

These festivities remind
us that regardless of our
differences...

We all
Celebrate!